By **Édith Pauly**
Photographs by **Sandrine Alouf**

THE BEST VINTAGE, ANTIQUE AND COLLECTIBLE SHOPS IN PARIS

The Little Bookroom New York

© 2008 The Little Bookroom
Production (US edition): Adam Hess
Additional translation (US edition): Tamar Elster

Originally published as Paris Déco
© 2008 Éditions Parigramme, Paris, France
Photographs © Sandrine Alouf, except for pages 228 to 240 © Sophie Compagne
Editors: Sandrine Gulbenkian and Clara Mackenzie
Artistic Direction: Isabelle Chemin
Layout: Sophie Compagne/Albert & cie
Translation: Anita Conrade
With the collaboration of Laurence Alvado, Lilith Cowan, Sylvie Nouaille, and
Mélanie Uleyn.

Pauly, Edith.
[Paris deco. English]
The best vintage, antique, and collectible shops in Paris / by Edith Pauly ;
photographs by Sandrine Alouf ; translated by Anita Conrade with Tamar Elster.
      p. cm.
ISBN 978-1-892145-73-4 (alk. paper)
1. Shopping—France—Paris—Guidebooks. 2. Antique dealers—France—Paris—
Guidebooks. I. Title.
TX337.F82P377513 2009
381'.10944361—dc22
                        2008041460

ISBN 978-1-892145-73-4

Published by The Little Bookroom
435 Hudson Street, 3rd Floor, New York, NY 10014
(212) 293-1643 Fax (212) 333-5374
editorial@littlebookroom.com
www.littlebookroom.com

Table of Contents

Introduction

 Antiques aficionados and rummagers of every stripe, call to mind dimly lit attics, trunks smelling of old leather, dusty cartons, and that indescribable tingle of suspense aroused by the idea of a hidden prize which has been lying there, biding its time, waiting for you to find it. Paris is a huge treasure trove, and if you follow the instructions we have mapped out for you, you might discover almost anything: a mariner's lucky charm, a butter churn, an armchair upholstered in leather gleaming with the rich patina of age, an Arne Jacobsen chair, a meerschaum cigarette holder, embroidered linen bed sheets, carved Indian doors, train station clocks, factory lockers … in other words, a jumble of objects as varied as those in a surrealist dream-poem. You're beginning to warm to the pleasures of the hunt, now, aren't you? Fortified with this windfall of Paris addresses, carefully selected to fulfill all your desires for travel into the past, you'll be equipped with what you need to search for the unknown, unexpected surprise, be it large or small. Paris still contains many mysterious secrets and magical places, which you'll discover, to your wonderment, as you explore its many second-hand stores, brimming with all sorts of decorative curiosities. At the rear of a courtyard or sheltered by a nineteenth-century arcade, in a Gothic stone basement or an ordinary looking shop, the addresses which follow will provide you with a cornucopia of delights at a variety of prices, and invariably with charm. If you linger for a word or two, the owners will ply you with stories. They love their trade, and will generously give advice and share stories about the wares they have to offer.

À l'Orientale

Arcades du Palais-Royal,
19-22, galerie de Chartres, 1ˢᵗ
Tel. 01 42 96 43 16
Métro: Palais-Royal-Musée-du-Louvre
Monday to Saturday, 11am to 7pm;
Sunday by appointment

■ Scents of cigar, incense, and tobacco float discreetly on the air: welcome to the kingdom of smoke. Though it is politically incorrect, the place is a favorite with many a dignitary from the Constitutional Council or Ministry of Culture, located nearby. Beneath the seventeenth-century colonnaded mall at Palais-Royal, Rakel Van Kote, an Israeli woman of Afghan extraction, stocks snuffboxes, pipes, manicure kits, canes, umbrellas, and curiosities, all of them antique. Her clientele, made up largely of collectors, includes Karl Lagerfeld and the great-grandson of Gustave Eiffel. The objects of their desire are arranged in stacks, sometimes precariously balanced one on top of the other, or overlapping in a charming puzzle of parts and pieces. True, the shop is pocket-sized, but it is located in one of Paris's most strollable neighborhoods. The renown of the proprietress is such that she often lends collectibles for use as movie props. For example, in the film *Molière*, Romain Duris puffs on a cigarette holder straight from this boutique.

À l'Orientale

11

Astier de Villatte

173, rue Saint-Honoré, 1st
Tel. 01 42 60 74 13
Métro: Tuileries or Palais-Royal-Musée-du-Louvre
Monday to Saturday, 11am to 7:30pm
www.astierdevillatte.com

■ Though the housewares, furniture, and china on offer here are not of venerable age, they have all been crafted with such attention to quality and elegance that one forgives them their youth. The creative concept could be summed up thus: to reintroduce poetry into the tradition—often bound by conventions—and endow it with additional grace. In a splendid setting, round-bellied Dutch chests of drawers sit alongside antique patterned dressers. Tables with ornately lathed black legs stand beside buffets displaying incredibly elegant plates—some of which are printed with flowers and grasses—complete the tableau, reminiscent of a Flemish painting. All the ceramics are produced according to the old-fashioned handbuilding technique, as was the rule before the casting process was introduced. Ivan Pericoli and Benoît Astier de Villatte also offer blank books and notebooks with covers inspired by antique molds. They compare their approach to that of an archeologist rather than that of antique dealers. Alongside the divine porcelain wares, fine furniture, and decorative objects, there are plastic ViewMasters from the 1960s, complete with souvenir slides, as well as antique postcards, adding a pleasant touch of kookiness to the shop's charm.

Astier de Villatte

15

Galerie Alexis Lahellec

14-16, rue Jean-Jacques-Rousseau, 1ˢᵗ
Tel. 01 42 33 36 95
Métro: Palais-Royal-Musée-du-Louvre or Louvre-Rivoli
Monday to Saturday, 12pm to 8pm
www.alexislahellec.com

Design & Things

22, rue du Pont-Neuf, 1ˢᵗ
Tel. 01 42 33 41 25
Métro: Les Halles or Pont-Neuf
Monday, 9:30am to 7pm;
Tuesday to Saturday, 9:30am to 8pm

■ Alexis Lahellec had a successful career as a jewelry designer before bursting onto the interior decoration scene, concocting baroque-looking objects, papier-mâché goblets, and furniture in wrought iron or wood. He's the designer behind the ultra-kitsch line of "Why" gadgets and accessories—another example of his dynamism and energy. However, in addition to being a powerhouse, Lahellec likes change. In 2007 he opened two vintage furniture shops in quick succession. The first, located on Rue Jean-Jacques-Rousseau, is a showroom for furniture, lighting, and accessories like vases and glassware, all dating from the 1950s and 60s, the golden age of Scandinavian modernism. Design & Things, Lahellec's second gallery, is stocked with similar items from Nordic sources, some of which were designed later, in the 1970s. The latter shop is located just a stone's throw from the Pont-Neuf, in a building which was once a grand nineteenth-century bank. (Be sure to visit the basement room, which is filled with treasures.) A mint-condition, vintage 1950 rosewood table, a Rietveld dining-room set, ceramics from Vallauris, Scandinavian decorative glass, matching Mathieu Matégot armchairs, a coffee table with an amazing mosaic top, and unusual light fixtures: a plethora of interior furnishings at prices that are quite affordable.

Galerie Alexis Lahellec / Design & Things

19

L'Œil du Pélican

13, rue Jean-Jacques-Rousseau, 1st
Tel. 01 40 13 70 00
Métro: Palais-Royal-Musée-du-Louvre or Louvre-Rivoli
Tuesday to Friday, 11am to 6:30pm;
Saturday, 3:30pm to 6:30pm
www.loeildupelican.fr

It's a curious name for an antique shop: The Pelican's Eye. An astronomer would probably guess it was a reference to the famous Pelican Nebula, but in fact, Françoise gave her shop the name for much more down-to-earth, purely geographical reasons: it happens to be located at the corner of a street named for the bird in question. As for the eye, the vintage trade demands good if not excellent judgement. Bitten by the second-hand bug back when she was a certified public accountant, Françoise operates on love at first sight. Seven years ago, she quit her day job and opened her shop to allow her passion to blossom. Most of the items on display date from the nineteenth or early twentieth centuries. Françoise skillfully combines unusual or surprising pieces, continually changing the arrangement. Here, a cast iron rabbit garden ornament lives peacefully alongside cardboard lawyer's or doctor's files. There are wooden horses that rock and others that roll, an ironing board, a gigantic porcelain mortar—in other words, a litany of one-of-a-kind antiques, like the enormous troika made to go on an early twentieth-century carousel. There's also a handsome assortment of luggage, suitcases, and even a plumber's toolbag, for those who appreciate travels through time.

L'Œil du Pélican

23

24

Rarissime

18, rue Saint-Roch, 1ᵉʳ
Tel. 01 42 96 30 49
Métro: Pyramides or Tuileries
Tuesday to Saturday, 12pm to 7:30pm

■ In the old days, market stalls attached themselves to the flanks of churches like oysters to a rock. This shop, dating back to the seventeenth century and a registered treasure of French architectural heritage, is one of the rare vestiges of that era. Though the surface area is tiny (about seventy square feet), proprietress Françoise Langlois would not leave it for anything in the world. Following studies at the Ecole du Louvre, she stocked her historically significant jewel box-sized store with the finest seventeenth-century knickknacks, statuettes, paintings, and drawings, sometimes making incursions into other periods. At the top of a miniscule staircase, on the second floor, there are even more items on display, and they are just as charming. However, don't expect to see much furniture here: the shop door is only about two feet wide. There are many small marvels, though. One of the most astonishing items on exhibit, a prize

Langlois find, is a delicate slipper, the survivor of a pair that was a gift from nineteenth-century pope Pius IX to an Italian noblewoman living in Paris.

Rarissime

27

As'Art

3, passage du Grand-Cerf, 2ⁿᵈ
Tel. 01 44 88 90 40
Métro: Étienne-Marcel
Tuesday to Saturday, 10am to 7pm
www.as-art.fr

■ Located in the heart of the Montorgueil neighborhood, the Passage du Grand-Cerf arcade itself, with its remarkable glazed roof (at 36 feet, the highest in Paris), is well worth a visit. The arcade, built in 1825, is now the home of several talented young designers and original interior decoration galleries. As'Art, spawned in 1991 as a way to involve a group of Kenyan craftsmen in a long-term development project, has since extended its concerns to other humanitarian causes. Consequently, nine years ago, this display and sales gallery was inaugurated. Currently, African design objects from today and yesteryear are collected in the bright space. On the ground floor, you'll see a series of contemporary design or craft pieces, alongside collectibles from the past. The sculpture, jewelry, fabrics, and furniture come chiefly from the southeast: Mozambique and South Africa. Downstairs, you'll enter the realm of antique African furnishings: wooden benches, royal stools, head rests, statuettes, and a wide range of utilitarian objects that will delight collectors and other connoisseurs of African art. More recent pieces like Maasai blankets and colorful Zulu basketry and weavings, using brightly insulated telephone wiring, can also be admired. The selection of Kisii soapstone vases, goblets, and carvings from Kenya is also of the very finest craftsmanship.

As'Art

31

NDIA

ANCE Co.Lᵀᴰ.

Bombay, 1919

AGENCIES

स्टनलस स्टील का उचा ब

HAMAM
TOILET SOAP

HAMAM

इमाम

इमाम

नड़ा...आबुन

MANGHOOMAL & SO

Rly. CATERERS
AND
CONTRACT

Rickshaw

7, passage du Grand-Cerf, 2nd
Tel. 01 42 21 41 03
Métro: Étienne-Marcel
Monday to Saturday, 11:30am to 7:30pm

Rickshaw Textiles

10, passage du Grand-Cerf, 2nd
Tel. 01 40 26 37 95
Métro: Étienne-Marcel
Tuesday to Saturday, 11:30am to 7:30pm

www.rickshaw.fr

■ Rickshaw is a bonanza for lovers of Indian craftsmanship. Most of the objects amassed here are antiques, found in markets all over the subcontinent. Mirrors, lacquered cups and bowls, old-fashioned coathooks, metal advertising signs, wooden typesetters' letters, glass mosaic lanterns…not to mention teak cabinets and even doors and woodwork from the nineteenth and early twentieth centuries: there's such a plenitude of fine objects, including some replicas of the more popular designs, that you'll feel as though you're walking through a bazaar.

Wander a little farther and explore the second shop, dedicated to fabrics. Quilts and bedspreads are on offer next to silks and richly brocaded and beaded saris. Brilliant cushions, throws, and curtains invite you to transform your bedroom into a maharajah's palace. The Bollywood lair is another possibility, for there's a huge selection of lurid movie posters.

Rickshaw

35

Rickshaw Textiles

37

Balouga

25, rue des Filles-du-Calvaire, 3rd
Tel. 01 42 74 01 49
Métro: Filles-du-Calvaire
Tuesday to Friday, 12:30pm to 7pm;
Saturday, 2pm to 7pm
www.balouga.com

■ Quality design is sure to have a trans-generational appeal. Grand-parents in search of the chairs, desks, or tables which made names for Jean Prouvé, Arne Jacobsen, Charles and Ray Eames, and Harry Bertoia need look no farther. Purists will delight in the vintage originals; the less discriminating will find excellent reproductions. Copies are proliferating as manufacturers put the classics back into production to meet a growing demand from the public. For instance, the legendary Verner Panton chair has just been reissued by Vitra, in Lilliputian format for the younger set. This shop is the brainchild of Véronique Cota, a former journalist, who changed careers after her children were born. After completing training in interior architecture at the famed École Boulle, she saw a mission for her-self: improve the variety of tastefully-designed furniture available for children. Recently, to fill out her catalogue, she has begun producing items designed by Matali Crasset and Mahmoud Akram.

Balouga

41

La Calinière

68, rue Vieille-du-Temple, 3ʳᵈ
Tel. 01 42 77 40 46
Métro: Saint-Paul
Open Daily, 3pm to 7pm

■ The love of Micheline's life is lighting, and it's an old romance: thirty years, and the flame is still burning bright, though she admits she is also fond of baubles and curiosities. Her favorite lamps are the enameled glass Art Deco masterpieces, available as ceiling- or wall-mounted lights or free-standing lamps, the work of such great glass craftsmen as Loys Lucha, Maxonade, and Fargue—when she can find them (Fargue is becoming a rare commodity). The ceiling of Micheline's store is literally aglow with chandeliers by Lalique, Verlys, and Sabino, but connoisseurs of Art Nouveau will also find temptations galore, with the likes of designers Daum, Muller, and Legras. In surroundings which are reminiscent more of an attic than a shop, cabinets, gueridon tables, and a wicker mannequin seem to be waiting for the day when someone will remember they are there. They give Micheline's lair an enchantingly old-fashioned feel.

La Calinière

45

Galerie Dansk

31, rue Charlot, 3rd
Tel. 01 42 71 45 95
Métro: Filles-du-Calvaire
Tuesday to Saturday, 2pm to 7pm
www.galeriedansk.com

■ Dansk may mean Danish, but the splendid items on display here were imported from throughout the Scandanavian countries. The gallery is the property of Jean-Loup Basset and Merete Degenkolw-Basset, lifelong aficionados of Scandinavian Modern-style furniture dating from 1950 to 1970. With the utmost taste, these two specialists have selected vintage originals of extraordinary quality. Often, these are veritable museum pieces, classics by the greatest names in design from Sweden, Norway, Denmark, or Finland: Hans Wegner, Alvar Aalto, and other visionaries. Armchairs, diningroom sets, lighting, tables, and desks are on display, as well as decorative ceramics and glassware. They've been collected with the help of a team in Copenhagen who also hunted down Krenit bowls and cups (made of a steel-enamel alloy), rarities by Herbert Krenchel which have never been reproduced. Every year, the gallery organizes an exhibit around a special theme: woman architects, the work of Hans Wegner or Verner Panton, to cite just a few of the subjects covered in the past. By appointment you may visit the vast warehouse in Montreuil, where even more furniture (some of it very large) is on show.

Galerie Dansk

49

Images et Portraits

35-37, rue Charlot (alternate entrance at
39, rue de Bretagne), 3rd
Tel. 06 65 23 95 03
Métro: Filles-du-Calvaire
Monday to Friday, 1pm to 7pm;
Saturday and Sunday, 10am to 7pm

■ The door of this shop, located in the Marché des Enfants-Rouges and filled with old photographs, leads us on a voyage into the charming world of the past. The usual snapshot formats are on display, most of them fairly small: prints straight out of old family albums, visual chronicles of events like weddings, vacations, picnics, and births, as well as anonymous yet familiar portraits. These are the images of simple joys chosen with amazing acuity by Fabien Breuvart. A shadow, a flaw, or an unusual composition are the criteria he judges by; the perfect photograph or famous artist's signature is practically banal to him. Collectors are not the only customers thumbing through these boxes full of prints that are left deliberately jumbled. Whoever walks in can embark on an adventure, guided by chance. Breuvart, formerly a photojournalist in Paris and New York, is a faithful advocate of film photography. He shoots studio portraits of neighbors and customers, one of the affordable pleasures most of us have forgotten.

Images et Portraits

photo
trouvée

53

Jérôme Lepert

106, rue Vieille-du-Temple, 3rd
Tel. 06 10 18 18 88
Métro: Filles-du-Calvaire
Tuesday to Saturday, 11:30am to 1pm and 3pm to 7pm

■ Aromas of metal, wood, and linseed oil pervade the shop, and yet it has a curious atmosphere of dignity and elegance, like an old-fashioned workshop or factory. Jérôme Lepert hunts down workbenches, Jieldé jointed desklamps, and floor lamps, as well as forms for making hats, carnival masks, or gloves. Apparently, his American colleagues call what he does "industrial archeology," which tickles Lepert's sense of humor. He may be passionate about these objects, but he doesn't take himself seriously. He's driven by some mysterious fervor to seek out factory and warehouse desks, tables, shelves, workbenches, clocks, lamps, and sometimes even machine parts. His tastes are shared by a number of loyal customers, including designer Philippe Starck. One of his major assets, in addition to his discriminating eye, is the quality of his restoration work. It's a simple trick for him to rewire an old lamp, and he's always careful to oil parts, for he knows that rust never sleeps.

ETOILES

Jérôme Lepert

57

Weber Métaux et Plastiques

9, rue de Poitou, 3rd
Tel. 01 42 71 23 45
Métro: Filles-du-Calvaire
Monday to Friday, 8:30am to 5:30pm
www.weber-france.com

■ Weber Métaux is a mecca for the do-it-yourselfer with a daunting shopping list. If you're looking for a good old-fashioned hardware store, take a trip to this venerable establishment, as old as the Eiffel Tower (1889). Its four floors contain an inventory of 225,000 items, from the unlikely to the indispensable. If you can't find it here, you won't find it anywhere. The basement aisles are lined with spools of copper wire, in every color imaginable; steel mesh, also available in a variety of colors; and an assortment of pipes and fittings. On the street level, where customers have long been welcomed, you will find the tool department. Upstairs, in fastenings, rows upon rows of drawers are filled with screws to suit every purpose. The third and top floor is dedicated to materials of various types: rolls of oilcloth, some of it self-adhesive, in solid colors, silver, or incredible patterns; felts of various thicknesses; an assortment of Bakelite; rolls of PVC film; synthetic glass; optical fiber; metal chain in various sizes, for sale by the meter; cardboard; foam . . . You name it.

12
1.5
1.8
2.5
4
6

1
1,4
1,6
2
2,2
5
5,5
4,5
6
7
8

Weber Métaux et Plastiques

61

Au Bon Usage

21, rue Saint-Paul, 4th
Tel. 01 42 78 80 14
Métro: Saint-Paul
Daily, 11am to 7pm, except Tuesday
www.aubonusage.com

■ Lovers of Thonet bentwood furniture are familiar with this shop, as are those who like folk art from the Black Forest, a region of Germany where it was customary to while away long winter evenings by carving linden-wood chests, boxes, crucifixes, and emblematic bears. These specialties of the house have been a family passion for over twenty-five years, and passed along to the son, who now manages the business. Guillaume Manuel took over the shop after training as an engineer, and gives his customers the benefit of his ongoing search for more masterpieces. It is certainly a pleasure to dream of owning the bentwood rocking chairs, loveseats, and tables. They were made in the 1880s in Austria by Michael Thonet, the first cabinetmaker to experiment with mass producing furniture or making it from kits. You'll also find charming framed prints and illustrations, as well as curiosities the proprietor could not resist. Don't miss the lovely collection of hand-turned boxwood objects, of infinite grace.

Au Bon Usage

65

UN PETIT LIVRE D'O

Au Petit Bonheur la Chance

13, rue Saint-Paul, 4th
Tel. 01 42 74 36 38
Métro: Saint-Paul
Daily, 11am to 1pm and 2:30pm to 7pm,
except Tuesday

■ School deportment records from the nineteenth century, jolly ceramic breakfast bowls, old-fashioned school supplies, enameled iron kettles: all of these objects, redolent of childhood, arouse nostalgic and tender memories. Everything is here, from the white paste smelling of almonds that children furtively taste, to individual slates and chalk, along with a complete set of Bibliothèque Rose children's books. Marie-Pia Varnier, a handbag designer, the daughter and niece of antique dealers, exults in childhood memories. She is also fond of sewing notions: mother-of-pearl buttons, ribbons and trim, monograms to label children's smocks. The teaching of the three R's has certainly changed, and those old primers and notebooks, with the multiplication tables on the back page, have their charm. Ditto for antique kitchen utensils. Miss Varnier has thus made nostalgia her stock in trade, and sifts through inventories from the 1930s to the 1970s in search of these themes, pre-ferring sets to single pieces. She delights in showing customers these Proustian remembrances of things past.

Au Petit Bonheur la Chance

69

CAMPHRE
PULVÉRISÉ

Aux Trois Singes

23, rue Saint-Paul, 4th
Tel. 01 42 72 73 69
Métro: Saint-Paul
Monday and Thursday to Saturday, 11am to 7pm;
Sunday, 2pm to 6:30pm

Also at Marché Paul-Bert, in the Saint-Ouen flea market

■ In a setting of undeniable charm, lush with plants and mosses, Sylvain Seron, a former landscape designer, offers a vast collection of antique garden decorations and tools: elegant Medici vases, watering cans which have seen many a springtime, romantic birdcages, a splendid pair of terracotta lions, figurative French roof ornaments, etc. You are also likely to happen upon numerous curiosities, craftsmen's workbenches and tools, Dutch chests of drawers, chandeliers, and more. Most of the items date from the eighteenth to early twentieth centuries. The shop, which opened only a few years ago, has enabled Sylvain Seron and his wife to combine their passion for antique hunting with the garden atmosphere which is so dear to them. The boutique interior alone is well worth a visit. It's so inviting, you will want to settle in for a nice long chat.

Aux Trois Signes

73

Cuisinophilie

28, rue du Bourg-Tibourg, 4th
Tel. 01 40 29 07 32
Métro: Saint-Paul
Tuesday to Friday, 2pm to 6:30pm

■ A "cuisinophile" is a person who collects kitchen utensils. Antique hunters of this type are irresistibly charmed by objects such as old stainless steel pitchers, enameled colanders, hand-cranked coffee grinders, spice jars, and butter churns. Annie Siquier is one of these enlightened ones, and her shopfront, with its beautiful peacock blue trim, is the gateway to a whole selection of the kind of utensils our grandmothers or great-grandmothers used every day. She chose this vocation on a whim, after having been both an art teacher and an artist. One morning, her neighbor, a shoemaker, told her he was retiring and abandoning the little shop downstairs from her apartment. Once she saw the tile flooring, it was a case of manifest destiny. The space is the perfect place to showcase the cooking utensils of yesteryear, along with functional tableware such as stoneware or porcelain dishes, bowls, and pitchers. A tireless

rummager, Annie is continually finding new pieces. She travels throughout France in search of rare and remarkable objects reminiscent of such delights as homemade jam, biscuits, and fresh butter.

MODESTO GASPAR, S. A.
SAGUNTO VALENCIA
ESPAÑA

Cuisinophilie

THÉ   CAFÉ   SUCRE

M'APPELLE
NPEINE
JE SUIS
EUSE MÉNAGÈRE
BREVETÉ S.G.D.G.

77

Fiesta

45, rue Vieille-du Temple, 4ᵗʰ
Tel. 01 42 71 53 34
Métro: Saint-Paul
Monday to Saturday, 12pm to 7pm;
Sunday, 2pm to 7pm
www.fiesta-galerie.fr

The property of an ex-TV producer and props manager, Fiesta honors, by its name, not only the party spirit, but also a type of American-made dinnerware well known to collectors. The brightly-glazed dishes have been a perennial favorite since the 1930s. This Parisian Fiesta, a den which has been around for almost twenty-five years, contains a savvy combination of curiosities predating the era of globalization, from typically American furniture to the great classics of European design from the postwar industrial boom. A figurine, standing on a table in a 1950s bouffant skirt, turns out to be a lamp. Mounted on the wall, a large gilded lamp from the 1940s spreads its metal foliage. Nearby, your attention is grabbed by a huge jukebox straight out of a Series B thriller. Classic metal signs, steering wheels from American cars, and impressive radio mikes from the 1950s are part of the collection. You could make your own movie, half

Rebel Without a Cause, half *American Graffiti*. And there's more than just Hollywood here: furniture by such iconic designers as Eero Saarinen, Alvar Aalto, Charles and Ray Eames, Bruno Matheson, and George Nelson is abundant. In an entirely different genre, a fragment of fencing bearing one of street artist Jérôme Mesnager's stenciled white silhouettes stands proudly in the window. The shop also leases items for movie sets.

Fiesta

81

Fuchsia

2, rue de l'Ave-Maria, 4ᵗʰ
Tel. 01 48 04 75 61
Métro: Saint-Paul
Tuesday to Sunday, 1pm to 7pm

■ There are linens hanging everywhere, from the rafters on down. You might think you'd just walked into a laundry. Before she became a passionate collector of household linens and took over this specialty shop, Élise Rodolphe, who studied art history for a time, loved fashion. She has diligently ferreted out pieces dating back to 1850 and as recent as 1950. She's an expert on lace from Calais, Le Puy, Alençon, Valenciennes, and Ireland, as well as monogrammed linen bed sets, tablecloths trimmed with delicate lace, curtains, and marvelous gowns. Her ribbons-and-trim section is well-stocked and enticing. Elise is happy to welcome customers and is generous with advice for them. Keep in mind that, in the old days, linen and lace were hand crafted, so each item is the only one of its kind. Prices vary, depending on rarity. Forewarned is forearmed . . .

Fuchsia

85

Les Touristes

17, rue des Blancs-Manteaux, 4th
Tel. 01 42 72 10 84
Métro: Hôtel-de-Ville
Tuesday to Saturday, 12pm to 7pm;
Sunday, 2pm to 7pm
www.lestouristes.eu

■ This is a thrilling shop to explore; it reawakens the pleasures of the hunt. Rummage through the cheerful cushions and old notebooks for tiny perfume flasks and druggist's eyedroppers, as if they were incredible treasures. After their Burmese, Chinese, and Moroccan adventures, Jérôme Gigot and Yann Gicquel have become acquainted with dealers in India. They bring back old embroidered saris, recycled as quilts from Rajasthani, ornate Uzbeki suzani embroidery, and splendid caftans. Here, the antiques are mingled with other items which are simply traditional. Old-fashioned armchairs are reupholstered with exotic fabrics imported from afar. Stationery, furniture, rugs, china, and perfumes from every land find a place in this collection, as long as they have that little touch of nostalgia, mostly for the years 1950 to 1970. In addition, our taste-ful tourists have released a collection of linens: tablecloths, cushions, bath towels, and curtains. The mood is delightfully old-fashioned. They also sell the wonderful Valobra brand of Italian soaps, whose elegant packaging makes them so very Riviera. The price range is as broad as the selection, and there are a number of small gift opportunities.

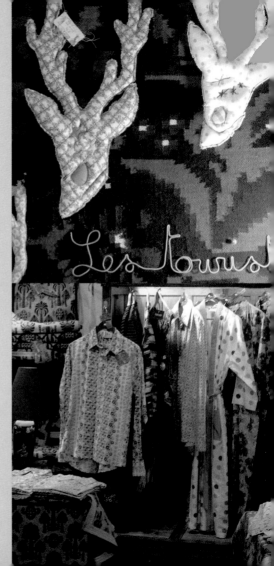

Les Touristes

89

Claude Nature

32, boulevard Saint-Germain, 5th
Tel. 01 44 07 30 79
Métro: Maubert-Mutualité
Tuesday to Saturday, 11am to 7pm
www.claudenature.com

■ Exotic butterflies with iridescent wings, beetles like precious jewels, small stuffed mammals, seashells with calligraphic markings: these are just a few of the surprises Claude Misandeau, a naturalist and former Deyrolle staff member (see page 111), has to offer you. Flesh out your zoology collection or your cabinet of curiosities with a small parakeet skeleton, perched on a dark wood branch. There are also marvels like minerals, geodes, animal skulls, centipedes, millipedes, and an abundance of arthropods both hairy and smooth, from the tarantula to the scorpion to the fossilized crab. In addition to the readymade collectibles, professional equipment (nets, pins, and display cases) is available to butterfly-hunting enthusiasts. Lepidopterist and novelist Vladimir Nabokov would have been delighted to browse this boutique.

Claude Nature

93

Dans l'air du temps

12, rue Lacépède, 5th
Tel. 01 42 17 06 39
Métro: Place-Monge
Tuesday to Friday (and sometimes Saturday),
11am to 7pm

■ Antique-hunting enthusiasts should be warned that it won't be easy to find this small store, hidden in the Rue Mouffetard neighborhood. Before Denise Achard opened Dans l'air du temps, she worked as an interior decorator, but she has never regretted her career switch. Here, she greets every customer with a smile, surrounded by piles of dishes and glasses galore. As you may surmise, housewares from the years 1940 to 1970 are the focus of her interest. She has a treasure trove of old sets of china, often displays Vallauris ceramics in a place of honor, and is well-acquainted with unusual objects like wire dish-drainers or cup-holders. You'll also find a selection of china cabinets in which to display the shop's offerings, refinished if necessary to make them more stylish. Household linens (old-fashioned tablecloths, sheets, and dish towels), ceiling lamps, dish racks which double as advertisements, and many other beloved finds make this time capsule a refuge for shoppers wishing to recreate the warmth of a family home redolent with memories.

Dans l'air du temps

97

La Tortue Électrique

7, rue Frédéric-Sauton, 5th
Tel. 01 43 29 37 08
Métro: Maubert-Mutualité
Tuesday to Saturday, 2pm to 6pm
www.tortue-electrique.com

■ Despite the whimsicality of the shop's name, La Tortue Electrique is a toy store for grownups, not children: adults who have maintained a passion for playthings and pastimes from their own childhood or that of their ancestors. This is the place to find vintage toys and games from the late nineteenth and early twentieth centuries, often displayed in their original packaging. European favorites like "Pêche à la ligne" and "Le Jeu de l'Oie" and global pastimes like checkers and mah-jong sets sit alongside singing tops, bowling pins, and toy firetrucks. You can even find a mint-condition 1952 stewardess costume still in its unopened packaging. The boutique, located in the heart of the Saint-Germain neighborhood, has a mezzanine level where proprietor Georges Monnier has set up his office. The former producer had been an amateur toy collector for years. He went professional after a business failure, when he had to start selling off his own collection to raise capital for a new start. Determined to live out his dreams, he dedicated himself to toy-collecting from that day on. He has been concentrating on the vintage years 1870 to 1910. After that, many small toy crafters closed down, as industrial toy factories began producing less refined playthings at a lower cost. Today, his clientele includes many collectors, of course, as well as museum curators: a guarantee of real value, even in the realm of fantasies and dreams.

La Tortue Électrique

101

Masala

44, rue Monsieur-le-Prince, 6th
Tel. 01 56 24 11 47
RER Luxembourg or Métro: Odéon
Tuesday to Saturday, 2pm to 7pm, or by appointment
www.masala.fr

■ Sandwiched between two shops on the Rue Monsieur-le-Prince, Masala is a jewel box filled to overflowing with adorable little marvels selected in remote Indian and Asian bazaars by Christine Berthollier, who used to direct TV programs for Canal +. Her knowledge of these cultures helps her to select each of the items she imports back to France one by one, rather than in batches, the way most dealers operate. The originality of the period pieces or folk-art specimens gleaned here and there is obvious. Clichés and unfaithful replicas are banished. Masala, which means "mixture of spices," is thus true to its name, offering a thrilling variety of objects to fall in love with, from the metal advertising sign to the Bollywood poster, and including incredible paintings, lithographs embroidered with pearls, and metal kitchenware items. Christine travels to the subcontinent twice a year to bring back a thousand and one of these irresistible marvels.

105

À la Mine d'Argent

108, rue du Bac, 7ᵗʰ
Tel. 01 45 48 70 68
Métro: Sèvres-Babylone
Monday to Friday, 10am to 6:30pm;
Saturday, 11am to 5pm
www.minedargent.com

■ This shop specializing in second-hand silverware has existed since the early twentieth century, and offers both solid silver and plated items. It's truly a silver mine: table settings, ladles, pie servers, teapots, coffeepots, and platters are available in profusion. A customer can either assemble a trousseau, as tradition once dictated, or simply find gifts for friends. This address, long known to the elegant ladies of the Sèvres-Babylone neighborhood, is one of the great classics of Parisian chic. It's a cornucopia of christening cups, napkin rings, knife rests, salt cellars, and, of course, knives, forks, and spoons. Perfectionists will be grateful for this opportunity to replace that dainty teaspoon which was thrown away by mistake. The shop also provides a range of additional services: appraisal of your collection, replating, engraving, a wedding gift registry, and even delivery abroad, upon simple request. This paradise will enchant worshippers at the altar of French gastronomy, amusing them with the incredible variety of flatware prescribed by etiquette for every purpose from soup to nuts: escargot forks, gumbo spoons, and crab claws, all designed to help us cope with our puzzling but delicious dishes. Feasting is not everything: it must be done in style.

À la Mine d'Argent

109

Deyrolle

46, rue du Bac, 7th
Tel. 01 42 22 30 07
Métro: Rue-du-Bac
Monday, 10am to 1pm and 2pm to 7pm;
Tuesday to Saturday, 10am to 7pm
www.deyrolle.fr

■ This venerable natural-history emporium, established in 1831, is a Paris landmark. Founder Jean-Baptiste Deyrolle and his son Achille were impassioned entomologists, and their trade began with the sale of equipment to specialists in their field. In 1866, Emile Deyrolle, one of the family's grandsons, developed the department which printed wall charts, and his main customer became the national school system. The instructive illustrations concerning every subject from human anatomy to botany to geography to civics are familiar to any Parisian born before 1970. Collectors and do-it-yourself naturalists will no doubt be delighted by the butterfly and beetle specimens from all over the world, minerals, fossils, and botanical collection equipment. Even more amazing is the taxidermy collection: an elephant calf, a lion, a horse, a bear, and many other specimens, often lent out as props for filmmaking. The antique display cases themselves, the originals, will fascinate visitors insensitive to the charms of natural history. Taken over by Prince Louis-Albert de Broglie, who merged it with his brand Le Prince Jardinier in 2001, the vast shop has now been fully restored. A veritable museum.

Deyrolle

113

Kin Liou

81, rue du Bac, 7th
Tel. 01 45 48 80 85
Métro: Rue-du-Bac or Sèvres-Babylone
Monday, 2pm to 6:30pm;
Tuesday to Saturday, 10:30am to 6:30pm

■ This tiny, elegant boutique is a magical and mysterious realm, where Monsieur Liou officiates with superb affability and erudition he is happy to share. The objects and small cabinets he sells are all antiques. Most of them are inspired by French colonial discoveries, but were made in France. This style, highly fashionable among nineteenth-century dandies, is the source of the many statuettes of African children, small lacquered bamboo tables from Asia, imitation Oriental bronzes (sometimes made into lamps by Kin Liou), delicate ivory chests with carved tops, sculptures of animals, and elegant woven baskets. All these objects bespeak a bygone era full of illusions about the empire, an era of both charm and depravity. Other objects, known as curiosities, supplement the collection: snuffboxes, inkwells, and terracotta busts. These smaller items, often displayed in cases or on shelves, share an undeniable originality and great quality in craftsmanship. If you'd like to see more furniture, ask Monsieur Liou to give you a tour of the warehouse located nearby.

Kin Liou

117

Et Puis c'est Tout

72, rue des Martyrs, 9th
Tel. 01 40 23 94 02
Métro: Pigalle
Monday, 2pm to 7pm;
Tuesday to Saturday, 12pm to 7:30pm;
occasionally Sunday, 3pm to 7:30pm

Apparently, all paths lead to vintage. Vincent Venin, once a master do-it-yourselfer and assiduous antique-hunter, worked first at a bank and then as a Club Med staff member. One day, he got a phone call from his brother, telling him that a shop right in his neighborhood had been put up for sale. In a flash, Vincent acquired the property and transformed himself into a professional dealer, bringing his wife along on the adventure. Many years have gone by since, but the passion and pleasure of plying this trade have stayed with the Venin couple. Today, they specialize chiefly in vintage 1950s to 1970s objects: clocks, bistro ashtrays bearing beverage ads, and old signs (like the legendary "carrots" that indicate tobacco shops), as well as old-fashioned metal office and factory cubbyholes, file cabinets, and lockers. There's also a selection of lighting fixtures. Vincent has an inventor's talent, and loves to assemble new pieces from the parts of old. One of the most amusing contraptions he has concocted is a floor lamp made from a beauty salon hair dryer.

Et Puis c'est Tout

121

Brokatik

2, rue de l'Hôpital-Saint-Louis, 10th
Tel. 01 42 40 10 34
Métro: Gare-de-l'Est or Colonel-Fabien
Wednesday to Friday, 12:30pm to 7pm;
Saturday and Sunday, 3pm to 7pm

■ Metal filing cabinets, industrial furnishings, wire mesh mail baskets, a stand for rubber stamps, a holepunch . . . If you added the shadow of the bored bureaucrat, in his gray smock, and the sound of him postmarking a letter, you'd think you'd stepped through a wrinkle in time to a post office from the 1950s. Eric Gosse, former art photographer, finds great pleasure in cultivating his philosophical independence. As he hunts for treasures from the 1950s and 1960s, he is continually feeding his curiosity. He's an intuitive buyer, and you can feel it, as you brush past the wooden physical therapist's table from the 1960s and catch a glimpse of the typical 1970s living room upstairs. Wending your way around the little end tables with twisted iron legs, which hold boxes full of promotional key rings, you are bound to marvel at the spirit and discipline of this collection—an engaging combination.

124

Brokatik

125

Loulou les Âmes Arts

104, quai de Jemmapes, 10th
Tel. 01 42 00 91 39 or 06 11 42 35 98
Métro: Jacques-Bonsergent
Wednesday to Sunday, 2pm to 7pm

■ "Atmosphère? Atmosphère? Est-ce que j'ai une gueule d'atmosphère?" You can't visit the Hôtel du Nord neighborhood, where Loulou is located, without recalling Arletty's fantastic lines from the film by Marcel Carné. Loulou, who worked first as a graphic artist and then as a photographer, discovered the antiques trade at a time in her life when she was adrift. She became attached, and finally dove in, opening her own shop. Today, she enjoys the treasure hunt as much as ever, and her selection, which includes pieces from the nineteenth century to the 1960s, reflects her enthusiasm. Vintage office furnishings, like the impressive 1930s dentist's cabinet with its myriad drawers, the dollhouse furniture, hat forms, shoes, accordions, industrial furnishing, and glassware: all these objects may come and go, depending on Loulou's poetic inspiration and the finds of the day. If you're curious enough to venture all the way to the back, you'll find the workshop where Loulou rewires lamps and other electrical gadgets, and creates original devices. This is a collection worth keeping an eye on.

SPATU

CISEAUX

Loulou les Âmes Arts

129

PLATE
35

PLATE
40

PLATE
45

PLATE
80

PLATE
90

PLATE
110

130

Au Progrès

11 bis, rue Faidherbe, 11ᵗʰ
Tel. 01 43 71 70 61
Métro: Faidherbe-Chaligny
Monday to Friday,
8:30am to 12pm and 1:30pm to 6pm
www.auprogres.net

Founded in 1873 and one of the landmarks of the Faubourg Saint-Antoine furniture district, this hardware emporium features an inventory of about 5,000 doorknobs, drawer pulls, ornamental newel caps, cabinet locks, period fittings, and cast iron or bronze fittings for French windows. The current proprietor, Georges Layani, whose father bought the business in 1960, spent his childhood wandering through the aisles lined with drawers and shiny old oak counters. He personally sees to it that the catalogue is complete, which sets this ironmonger apart. There is such a huge selection that Georges admits there are still some unopened boxes in his storeroom; he has never quite used up all the items in his inventory. It was Layani the elder who started the custom of displaying a sample of the contents of a drawer on the drawer front, to make it easier to serve customers. Don't miss the big Yankee-made cash register, vintage 1908 but still being used. It's definitely worth a look. A cult destination.

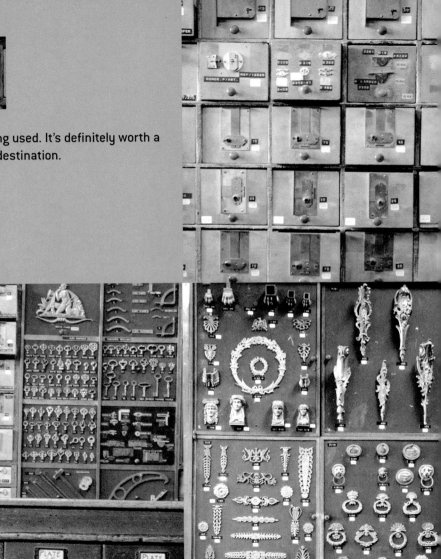

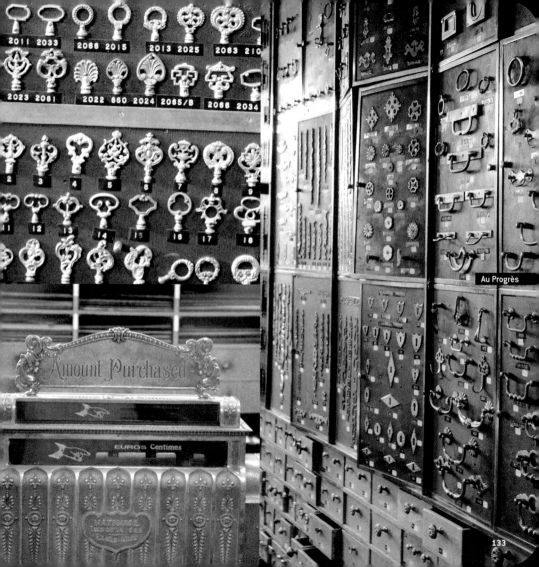

Au Progrès

133

Carouche

18, rue Jean-Macé, 11th
Tel. 01 43 73 53 03
Métro: Charonne
Monday, 2pm to 7pm;
Tuesday to Saturday, 11am to 7pm
www.carouche.typepad.com

■ Caroline Giraud is almost always wearing a broad smile. An antique lover practically from the cradle, she first studied art history and tried a career in photography before starting a company which rented vintage automobiles for film shoots and other events. You may find the idea curious, but for a collector's daughter, it was only natural. Yielding to her passion for the hunt, Caroline then decided to open her own antiques shop . . . but in an original way, of course. Her colorful den is more than just a sales point for objects from the past: she restores them, reinterprets them in form or function, and might even go ahead and repaint them in contemporary hues, if she feels that would be an improvement. She stocks vintage Fifties light fixtures, cabinets, and accessories; industrial furniture including metal or wooden lockers and filing cabinets; and desks. But she also exhibits a strange copper sterilizing unit for medical equipment,

movie theater seats which, though unlikely to be comfortable, have a great deal
of charm, and Bavarian porcelain teacups
and saucers, all with different designs.
She completes her inventory with objects
from more or less well-known designers,
which she delights in combining with salvaged materials often found in northern
France and Belgium. And here's a little
secret: she'd like to start introducing her
own creations at her shop.

Aile postérieure

LI-LOUP

Carouche

137

Le Château
de ma mère

108, avenue Ledru-Rollin, 11ᵗʰ
Tel. 01 43 14 26 03
Métro: Ledru-Rollin
Monday, 2:30pm to 7:30pm;
Tuesday to Saturday, 11:30am to 7:30pm

■ A specialty second-hand shop which also occasionally serves as a consignment store for the bobo (bourgeois bohemian) mothers in the neighborhood. They deposit their little monsters' surplus toys, outgrown strollers and prams, and other nursery accessories, which their fellow moms are delighted to find at a discount price. Catherine Palhalmi invented this original concept. As you browse the selection, where antiques mingle with more recent second-hand items, you will find some charming vintage pieces, especially among the cribs. There's also a child-sized barber's chair, an American classroom desk with a cast-iron frame, and a rocking swan from the 1950s. Nursery lamps, mirrors, wall decorations, and many other marvelous little accessories await you. A fascinating collection of old-fashioned high chairs overlooks the racks of children's clothing. Sweetness, charm, and simplicity: the taste of childhood.

Le Château de ma mère

Complément d'objet

11, rue Jean-Pierre-Timbaud, 11th
Tel. 01 43 57 09 28
Métro: Oberkampf
Wednesday to Saturday, 2pm to 8pm;
Tuesday by appointment
www.complementdobjet.com

■ Imagine a solid collection of floor lamps and ceiling fixtures, add some chairs, coffee tables, and small cabinets, a sprinkling of vases and other accessories, and you have some idea of what awaits you here. The two-floor shop, with a vaulted cellar, is packed with objects, often designer originals. From a small office in the back, Patrice Rotenstein keeps watch. He's not the chatty type, unless you get him started on his passion: repairs and restoration. A former electronics student, he has true genius as a tinkerer. His favorite subject is vintage lighting from the 1930s to the 1980s. Gilded deco wall-mounted fixtures, desk lamps, ceiling lamps, and even table lamps are available in profusion, with creations by Pierre Guariche, Gras or Ravel brand industrial lighting, or Gilles Derain wall sconces. To vary the pleasures, there are also small tables designed by Alvar Aalto, Prouvé chairs, and other design classics, in the shop or in the storeroom nearby, which can be visited by appointment.

Complément d'objet

Les Curieuses

4, rue Oberkampf, 11th
Tel. 01 47 00 97 65
Métro: Filles-du-Calvaire
Monday, 2pm to 7:30pm;
Tuesday to Saturday, 10:30am to 7:30pm
www.lescurieuses.com

When Bruno Tin and David Gaillard opened their brand-new showroom, with its taupe and gray color scheme, they opted to combine elegance and refinement. David, whose parents were antique dealers, began to ply the trade when he was only fifteen years old. Not long ago, he was a dealer in Rouen, and still owns a 4,000-square-foot warehouse in Normandy filled to the rafters with merchandise. Customers and visitors to the Paris store are welcomed by the owners amid the vintage industrial cabinets, farm or monastery dining tables, school desks, metal toys, rocking horses, and wrought iron children's bedsteads. Fabric lovers will be delighted by the quality and quantity of the bedlinen selection, dyed in the house colors. There are also lace bedspreads and splendid trousseaus for new brides. Contemporary fabrics designed by Dominique Kieffer can be made into cushions or curtains by the house seamstress.

Other original creations arouse curiosity: ceramics by Kim Heyong or Vincent Bellanger, and the panels with figurative or material motifs, which can be made to order. Les Curieuses can also be hired as an interior design and contracting team. Parting advice: go down the tiny staircase carefully—it's a bit steep.

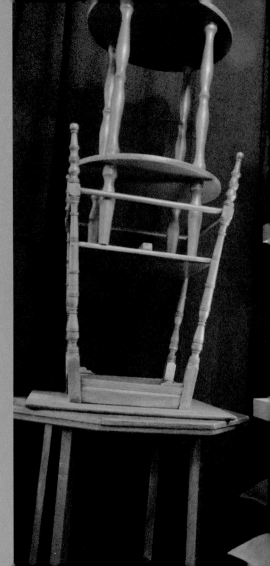

Les Curieuses

149

Les Frères Nordin

215, rue du Faubourg-Saint-Antoine, 11th
Tel. 01 43 72 38 35
Métro: Faidherbe-Chaligny
Monday to Saturday,
9:30am to 12:30pm and 2:30pm to 6pm

■ Long famous as the furniture district, the Faubourg Saint-Antoine was where all the cabinetmakers, finishers, bronzesmiths, and other craftsmen were located. Times have changed, of course, but a few of them still maintain shops on the street or in the many alleys which have always made the Faubourg special. For instance, if you duck into the courtyard that runs alongside the Nordin brothers' furniture shop (for they are also cabinetmakers), you'll reach their hardware store. It's a regular beauty salon for wood, where you can get expert advice about the mysterious oils, unguents, and varnishes these specialists have developed to beautify, maintain, restore, or give a shiny finish to wooden furniture or flooring. The shelves contain tins and jars of miracle products: French varnish, color-coordinated fillers to plug up the pores in the wood, linseed oil, poppyseed oil, fish-based glues, bitumen, "popote" (a magical conditioner familiar to all antiques-restorers), gum tragacanth of various types, and bees-wax polish. You will also find all the other tools of the refinishing trade: steel wool of various weights, cotton and polishing brushes, and, of course, paintbrushes for specialty tasks. Amiably offered advice paired with the exceptional quality of the products offered make this shop a must-see.

Les Frères Nordin

153

La Maison

3, ruc Neuve-Popincourt, 11ᵗʰ
Tel. 01 48 06 59 47
Métro: Parmentier
Tuesday to Friday, 12pm to 7pm;
Saturday and Sunday, 2pm to 7pm

■ Here, eras intentionally intersect, just as affinities do. This shop is an adventure launched by two young women. One was a graphic artist, the other an executive assistant. Their antique addiction was beginning to spin out of control, so Dominique and Eléonore quit their jobs, pooled their energies, and created La Maison. As experts on the 1950s, '60s, and '70s, they shop for love-at-first-sight vintage, the type of things that strike them as absolutely irresistible. And they find it: small pieces of furniture, ceiling suspension lights, a tidy little kitchen cabinet, a metal one: all seem to wink at the browsing shopper. An enormous Continental brand fan from the 1950s rules the center of the store. The plaster-block shelving along the side wall displays a car stereo that plays 45s, plates, glasses, and pitchers. Fortysomethings will chuckle at the sight of the Mobil gasoline keepsake drinking glasses from their childhood—totems which make this Maison such a unique place.

Trolls et Puces

1, rue du Marché-Popincourt, 11th
Tel. 01 43 14 60 00

Belle Lurette

5, rue du Marché-Popincourt, 11th
Tel. 01 43 38 67 39
Métro: Parmentier

Tuesday to Friday, 12pm to 7pm;
Saturday and Sunday, 2pm to 7pm

■ Two shops in one. These two dealers are totally independent; the only thing separating their shops was a steel shutter which, wisely, they immediately lifted. Now, without even realizing it, the customer zig-zags from one shop to the other. On the Trolls et Puces side, you may catch a whiff of paint: craftspeople at work on a refinishing job. You wander past salvaged wooden shutters, an old traffic light, metal fittings, and metal grillwork shelving, but you'll also notice a handsome crystal chandelier. Three steps away, at Belle Lurette, there are cabinets from grain shops or notions merchants, an adorable chest of drawers and a Second Empire divan, walls covered with pictures: such a profusion of pieces that they literally have to be stacked. Keep your eyes peeled or you'll miss something, there's such a variety of goodies. At first glance, you may be puzzled about which shop an item belongs to, but if you check closely, you'll see a little tag indicating that detail. In any case, the mistresses of the shop know their merchandise by heart.

Trolls et Puces

98.

Belle Lurette

163

Caravane Emporium

22, rue Saint-Nicolas, 12th
Tel. 01 53 17 18 55

22, rue Saint-Nicolas, 12th
Tel. 01 53 17 18 55

Caravane Chambre

19, rue Saint-Nicolas, 12th
Tel. 01 53 02 96 96
Métro: Ledru-Rollin

Open Tuesday to Saturday, 11am to 7pm
www.caravane.fr

After an apprenticeship with the international gallery and antiques house Didier Aaron, Françoise Dorget did a long stint as head of Etamine, the famous fabrics maker of the 1980s. Leaving the corporate world behind, she embarked on a tour of the planet's bazaars and marketplaces. From her travels, this indefatigable explorer gleans fabrics and everyday utensils made according to the traditional methods of the people she visited. The name of her Paris shop, Caravane Emporium, is borrowed from that of the Indian state cooperatives. Her own marketplace is a stage for objects which, though heterogeneous, undeniably have a poetry in common. The textiles and implements are not very old, but the techniques used to make them are usually ancient. The shop feels like an old colonial

trading post, stocked with weavings from Morocco, iron cookware from India, an odd hassock made from a recycled tire, carpets, small lamps, and fabrics of spectacular beauty. However, in addition to the merchandise from distant lands, the little gallery with blue-tinted whitewashed walls contains European wares, some which are even contemporary: a hassock made of a bale of straw upholstered in transparent plastic, and a movable wall sconce with a long vermilion wire. Engaging freely with contrast, Françoise creates bridges between different worlds, with empathy and refinement.

Caravane Emporium / Caravane Chambre

167

Les Modernistes

2, rue Théophile-Roussel, 12th
Tel. 06 26 12 37 41
Métro: Ledru-Rollin
Thursday to Saturday, 10am to 7:30pm;
Sunday, 10am to 2pm
www.lesmodernistes.com

Chancelia Debraux champions the decades from the 1950s to the 1970s, and, more generally, the twentieth century. Her shop with its big bay windows, a short hop away from the Marché d'Aligre and its small flea market, offers design classics created by such great names as Pierre Guariche, Pierre Paulin, Jean-Michel Wilmotte, and René-Jean Caillette. In these spacious surroundings, which resemble a gallery more than a second-hand store, lighting and furniture are arranged with sobriety. Chancelia's favorite reference is the famous Salon des Arts Ménagers— a French housewares trading show—which, from 1923 into the 1980s, was the showcase for every possible novelty in home furnishings. In this resolutely contemporary setting, Chancelia Debraux organizes a yearly exhibit on a special theme. In the past, she has done "Fifty 1950s chairs," and "Forty pieces chosen by ceramicists Andrée and Michel Hirlet

(1962-2005)." She has also featured "Silk-screens and paintings by Ado Sato," a great Japanese artist. As an enlightened and generous scholar, Chancelia welcomes today's great designers into her shop on a regular basis. Perhaps it's a source of inspiration for them.

Les Modernistes

Les Portes du Monde

166, boulevard du Montparnasse, 14th
Tel. 01 43 35 01 02
RER Port-Royal or Métro: Vavin
Tuesday to Saturday, 11:30am to 7pm,
or by appointment
www.portesdumonde-paris.com

■ The idea is original, to say the least, and the experiment is a daring one. Attuned to the symbolism of the door and the concept of "welcome" associated with it, Croisine Lebas was dismayed to see its design being uniformized. As a result, Croisine chose to specialize in antique, exotic doors, large and small. Some of them are painted, others are carved. Some are made of teak, others of cedar. Most of the doors date from the eighteenth and nineteenth centuries, and were found in India, Pakistan, Morocco, and China. There are a few architectural elements as well: porticos, columns, mashrabiyas, and windows are exceptions to the door rule, and find a place in the selection. The warehouse-studio can be visited by appointment, should you wish to explore the collection further. It is possible to adapt all the models displayed in the shop for installation in a Paris apartment.

Les Puces de Vanves

Avenue Marc-Sangnier,
Avenue Georges-Lafenestre, 14th
Métro: Porte-de-Vanves
Saturday and Sunday, 7am to 1pm on Avenue Marc-Sangnier;
Saturday and Sunday, 7am to 3-5pm (depending on the vendor)
on Avenue Georges-Lafenestre
www.pucesdevanves.typepad.com

■ The Vanves flea market is allegedly the oldest in Paris: written records of its existence date back to the late eighteenth century. This famous second-hand market in the southern part of town is now spread along Avenues Marc-Sangnier and Georges-Lafenestre. Every weekend of the year, some 380 merchants simply unpack their wares on the sidewalk. Large pieces of furniture are rare, but there's a great quantity of china, candlesticks, mirrors, and other objects. On Avenue Georges-Lafenestre, between the many stands with a varied inventory, Jean-Pierre Koch specializes in eighteenth- to twentieth-century silverware. Everything he sells is solid silver. Nearby, at Françoise Warion's stand, named La Route du Chineur, you'll find small furniture items, Second Empire clocks, 1960s lighting sconces, mirrors from the 1920s and '30s, all to be admired at leisure. On Avenue Marc-Sangnier, check Dan Schanus's collection of accessories, china, and cabinets, at Le Grenier du Particulier. A hop, skip, and a jump away, in a totally different style, Nicole Andrei specializes in industrial cabinets and workbenches. On a fine day, a visit to the Vanves flea market is an exhilarating experience. There's atmosphere galore: the dealers' repartees and rudeness are part of the folklore, as are the rowdiness and laughter.

Les Puces de Vanves

179

FONDÉE EN 1847 PAR

PAR
DRA
BRUXELLES

En Vente ici
Vernis
Bois

Spéciaux
pour le

CHÊNE CLAIR

NOIR JAPONAIS

40°

BERGER

Le Temps Suspendu

103, rue du Théâtre, 15th
Tel. 01 45 75 80 67
Métro: La Motte-Picquet-Grenelle
Monday to Saturday, 2pm to 7pm

■ Between Lost Time and Time Regained, there is Suspended Time, the moment when past and present mingle and the future is approaching . . . but very, very slowly. This shop is a place to linger, examining the assortment of more or less vintage toys and games, pencils, schoolbooks, picture books, and dollhouse china, bound to please those who feel sentimental about a vanished childhood. Objects from the nineteenth and twentieth centuries, some of them everyday implements for our parents or grandparents, have been collected from individuals. There are china dishes, small pieces of furniture, wicker trunks, and pictures, as well as tiny perfume flasks and splendidly decorated boxes. All these deliciously old-fashioned objects will enrapture those nostalgic for the Belle Epoque and its Art Nouveau extravagance or the soaring exuberance of Roaring Twenties Deco. Should these sorts of dreams leave you cold

as marble, never fear: more recent treasures with just as much charm are also on
display.

Le Temps Suspendu

183

Au Présent du Passé

36, ruc Davioud, 16ᵗʰ
Tel. 01 42 24 06 08
Métro: Ranelagh
Monday, 3pm to 7pm;
Tuesday to Saturday, 11am to 7pm

■ This is a neighborhood second-hand store, with a charming personality that's a touch provincial. Monique Kermel was long a bookseller, before yielding to her passion. There are a few guéridon tables and cabinets where china, silverware, and glassware sets are displayed. Garden furniture, paintings, prints, curios, and household linens complement the large variety of treasures, which are topped off by an adorable little collection of antique children's furniture: armchairs, tables, and high chairs, straight out of a Victorian nursery. Collectors of antique dolls will find tiny tea sets in porcelain or faïence, as well as the type of dollhouse furniture connoisseurs covet. Kermel's intuitive understanding of art and literature has served her well.

LES ALBUMS ROSES
LE CHAT BOTTÉ

Au Présent du Passé

187

Aux Salles de Bains rétro

27, rue Benjamin-Franklin, 16th
Tel. 01 47 27 14 50
Métro: Trocadéro
Tuesday to Saturday, 11am to 6pm

By appointment:
29-31, rue des Dames, 17th
Tel. 01 43 87 88 00
Métro: Place-de-Clichy

www.sbrparis.com

■ Perhaps you dream of taking bubble baths in a marble, zinc, or cast iron tub. Or would you simply like to find antique faucet fittings for your sinks? Aux Salles de Bains Rétro is the place to go for either of these desires. In addition to tubs, you'll find small portable Belle Epoque showers, dolphin-themed faucetry, Victorian flowered porcelain sinks, brackets, light fixtures, bottles, flasks, pedestal sinks...everything here is vintage. Nevertheless, there are a few reproductions of old-fashioned models available. Among the treasures not to be missed is the honey-colored onyx bathtub in which the famed Marquise de la Païva pampered herself before hosting her Second Empire salons. The patience and skill of Nicolas Beboutoff are another legendary attraction of the house. Its proprietor for thirty years now, he is a peerless restoration expert. No element of vintage plumbing can resist him. The sixteenth-arrondissement address is the showroom for important pieces, but the shop on the Rue des Dames and the warehouse on the outskirts of Paris are also spectacular sights to see. This dealer is an institution in the world of interior decoration—even for movie set designers, who are always looking for remarkable accessories.

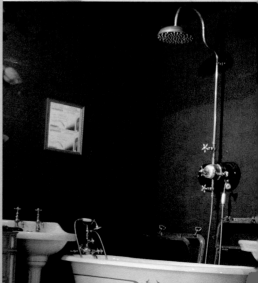

Aux Salles de Bains rétro

191

Antiquités Delacroix

67, place du Docteur-Félix-Lobligeois, 17th
Tel. 01 42 29 31 36
Métro: Rome or Brochant
Monday to Saturday, 10:30am to 7pm

■ Endowed with excellent instincts and taste, Agnès Delacroix, the proprietress of this shop, selects pieces from the eighteenth to twentieth centuries. A purist, she loathes copies, and has banished them from her domain. Trained in the craft of gilding, Ms. Delacroix has a studio (where she does restoration work for some clients) in the back of the shop, which looks out onto the charming little church Sainte-Marie-des-Batignolles, built 1826-1839, just across the street. Its colonnaded façade is reminiscent of a Greek temple, and it is one of the rare churches without a steeple. Agnès' capacious shop window, ingeniously circular, displays lovingly-discovered treasures: candelabras, painted metal chests, china, and a few framed paintings and prints, as well as furniture. A tall cabinet stands at the rear of the store, its doors open wide to reveal all manner of baubles on the shelves within. This is the bric-a-brac corner, where customers are welcome to rummage and explore. It's just as much fun as unpacking a mysterious old trunk you've just found in the back of the attic.

Antiquités Delacroix

195

De l'autre côté de la Butte

5, rue Muller, 18th
Tel. 01 42 62 26 06
Métro: Château-Rouge
Tuesday to Saturday, 2pm to 7pm;
Sunday, 3pm to 6pm

Stand at marché Vernaison,
at the Saint-Ouen flea market
(Stand 178, allée 8)

■ The hidden side of the Montmartre neighborhood hosts a hodgepdge of a second-hand store and that's just the way the owner likes it. Julien Brisedoux, who settled "on the other side of the hill" about ten years ago, delights in offering the inhabitants of the neighborhood and adventuresome wanderers a selection of cabinets and chairs, unusual works of art, a variety of curios, and jumbles of items purchased from individuals, dealers, or auctions. Formerly an economist and city planner, Brisedoux used to organize seminars for Franco-American scholars, as well as amateur freshwater fishing expeditions. His taste for objects which have stewed "in their own juices" finally drove him to open his own store. State-of-the-art airplane models made by an elderly gentleman who lives near Le Bourget airport, piles of old linen sheets from a boarding school, mantelpiece mirrors, collections of old postcards, magazines, chandeliers, café glasses, and even a Brazilian cabaret headdress made of white feathers and glass beads are among the objects which found their way into his possession. An antique hound's dream, especially due to the more than reasonable prices. Beware of temptations.

VOUS ÊT...
EN RETA...

De l'autre côté de la Butte

L'Objet qui parle

86, rue des Martyrs, 18th
Tel. 06 09 67 05 30
Métro: Abbesses
Monday to Saturday, 1pm to 7:30pm

■ Certain objects speak of the past, of poetry, of vanished worlds, of childhood and mysteries. Guillaume and Dominique are gifted with the ability to detect them. A small stuffed crocodile, incredible ex-voto offerings of crucifixes in bottles, glass bells: every object attracts your gaze and inspires a smile. When you step over the threshold, you leave Paris for an unknown destination, a magician's lair, a curiosity cabinet, or a long-abandoned attic. With its brick walls patched here and there with plaster, or covered with paneling painted in tropical Brazilian favela colors, this boutique is instantly engaging. You'll also find rural furniture, sunburst mirrors—usually Second Empire, coffee tables and leather chests, majestic chandeliers. This enchanting shop should be visited as much for the journey into the past it provides as for the objects it displays.

L'Objet qui parle

Pages 50/70

15, rue Yvonne-Le-Tac, 18th
Tel. 01 42 52 48 59
Métro: Abbesses
Tuesday to Saturday, 2pm to 7pm;
Monday and Sunday by appointment
www.pages50-70.com

Known to professionals and amateurs alike, this address is entirely devoted to the remarkable creations of the second half of the twentieth century. Owner Olivier Verlet is a discriminating buyer whose selection contains nothing but museum pieces, classic examples of fine design: furniture by Charles and Ray Eames, Joe Colombo, Pierre Paulin, Mies van der Rohe, and Eero Saarinen, an Arne Jacobsen champagne bucket—not to mention ceramics crafted by Roger Capron and Marcel Guillot, and Italian light fixtures. Other accessories on offer here include serving dishes and table settings, glassware, and the occasional thunderbolt, like the splendid Mathieu Matégot wall hanging, a rare and surprising object. Though it's unusual, the owner's high standards for design quality are not reflected by the prices, which are quite fair.

Pages 50/70

207

Tombées du camion

15-17, rue Joseph-de-Maistre, 18th
Tel. 06 62 07 20 87
Métro: Blanche
Monday to Friday, 1pm to 8pm;
Saturday and Sunday, 11am to 8pm
tombéesducamion@hotmail.fr

■ The shop that goes by this name, a little joke about stolen goods, is an Ali Baba's cave of treasures, half curiosity shop, half second-hand store, filled to the rafters with anachronistic objects from the past. The resident genie, Charles Mas, used to ply his trade in the usual way, buying and selling items depending on what he found. But one day, he realized that there was not one single store where antique hunters could procure a whole series of a single item. As a result, he decided to focus on buying batches when factories closed (mainly in France), giving rise to an absurd and poetic catalogue of old-fashioned implements which have never been used. Everything is displayed in little wooden cubbyholes: mother-of-pearl buttons, Bakelite switches, dolls' eyes, policemen's whistles, perfume-bottle labels, watch faces, billiard balls, cricket cages, engravers' plates, wooden typefaces, and even a great deal of costume jewelry from the 1970s. Dive into this jumble of twentieth-century relics to compose a mysterious individual universe for yourself.

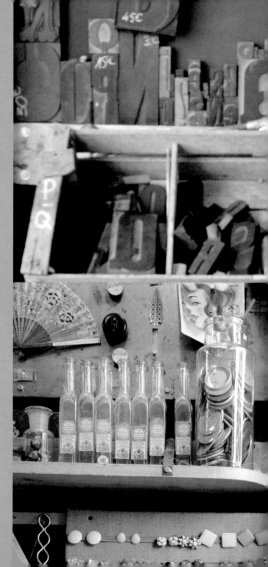

Tombées du camion

Zut

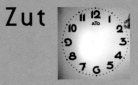

Frédéric Daniel Antiquités
7-9, rue Ravignan, 18th
Tel. 06 82 67 81 77
Métro: Abbesses
Wednesday to Saturday,
11am to 1pm and 4pm to 7pm;
Sunday, 11am to 1pm
www.antiquités-industrielles.com

■ In this shop, with its suave slate-gray trim, the collection displayed by Frédéric Daniel seems timeless, as if suspended, awaiting the magic moment when a customer will give an object new life. Clocks that seem to have come straight from a railway station, a plump cast iron Michelin Man, a traffic signal, metal furniture, industrial lamps, film projectors, a globe, and heaps and heaps of clocks, like Sleeping Beauties, bide their time until their Prince or Princess Charming comes. As a specialist in "industrial antiquities and urban objects," Frédéric is blissfully independent of market trends. He prizes his freedom of choice, reminding the listener that he works for love, for sheer pleasure. In fact, he named his boutique "Zut" as an homage to a café which once stood on the same street, in its time famous as a meeting place for anarchists. It was owned by one Frédéric Gérard (the Frédéric character in *Quai des Brumes*), and was

closed by the authorities in 1903 following a brawl. In modern times, Zut has somewhat anarchistic hours, but Frédéric usually tapes a card with his cell-phone number on the door, and he's never far away.

Zut

215

Antiquités-Curiosités

62, boulevard de Ménilmontant, 20th
Tel. 06 83 12 70 75
Métro: Père-Lachaise
Tuesday and Thursday to Saturday,
usually 11am to 7pm

This small shop is a well-kept secret, nestled between the hipster bars and restaurants on the boulevard near Père-Lachaise Cemetery. Proprietor Jean-Louis Demange used to work as a professional photographer, but he was an antiques hound who loved to hunt through flea markets, and once he had sniffed out enough vintage cameras, he ended up opening a stand at the Saint-Ouen flea market. Many travels and changes later, he is an antique dealer in a neighborhood on the verge of gentrification. On the strength of his whims, he may bring back Scandinavian furniture, bronze sculpture, industrial furnishings, architects' drafting tables, Perzel lamps, or globes. The objects from 1900 to 1970 displayed in his boutique are varied, original, and always excellent value for the price. Other dealers often visit to check on his finds. Careful, it's a good idea to phone before dropping in.

Antiquités-Curiosités

219

Agapè

91, avenue Jean-Baptiste-Clément
92100 Boulogne-Billancourt
Tel. 01 47 12 04 88
Métro: Boulogne-Jean-Jaurès
Tuesday to Saturday, 11am to 7pm
www.agapedeco.com

■ Julie Isoré hunts down, transforms, and restores pieces from a number of different periods and styles. Like a virtuoso, she can strike a note of harmony between salvaged, stripped-down materials and the neo-industrial esthetic, without losing any of the warmth of a cozy home. Magic dwells in her white-paneled shop with the patterned cement-tile floor. Danish modern teak furniture typical of the 1960s converses with a crystal chandelier; a bull's-eye window overlooks a Dutch table. A number of cubbyholes and filing cabinets from factories or craftsmen's shops have been attractively restored by the proprietress. This young woman with astounding energy admits that she has a predilection for white and shades of gray, noticeable in the clocks and chests of drawers. Because she has a taste for detail, she has also found argentite candlesticks, wedding bells, and all sorts of other witty conversation pieces. Julie also takes on a number of interior decorating jobs, and knows how to give pizzazz to old furniture forgotten in an attic or basement.

Agapè

223

XXO

78, rue de la Fraternité
93230 Romainville
Tel. 01 48 18 08 88
Monday to Friday, 9am to 6:30pm
www.xxo.com

■ Every self-respecting ad or set designer is familiar with this incredible warehouse, with its surface area of over 35,000 square feet. Founded in 1998 by three former dealers from the Vanves and Saint-Ouen flea markets, this "design mecca" is the home of the largest vintage collection in Europe, with an inventory of nearly 2,500 pieces (desks, lamps, bathroom furnishing, and even telephones). All of the objects are available for sale or lease in this space which is half furniture warehouse, half retailer. You'll admire mint-condition Sixties and Seventies classics, the furniture and accessories from the biggest brands in the art of design (Knoll, Artemide, and Kartell) and the most famous and innovative designers: Pierre Paulin, Philippe Starck, Fernando and Umberto Campana, Mourgue, Charles and Ray Eames, Fritz Hansen, and Herman Miller, as well as some other Italian stars. Monochromatic plastic, stylish leather,

aluminum, wood . . . Lovers of design will
go wild.

Les Puces de Saint-Ouen

Rues des Rosiers, Jules-Vallès, Biron, Paul-Bert
93400 Saint-Ouen
Renseignements au 0892 705 765
Métro: Porte-de-Saint-Ouen or Porte-de-Clignancourt
Open Saturday to Monday, 9am to 6pm
www. parispuces.com

The Saint-Ouen tourist bureau offers four guided flea-market tours per year
Tel. 01 40 11 77 36
Downloadable audio guide available in mp3 format at www.pocketvox.com.

■ Like its London cousin at Portobello Road, the Saint-Ouen flea market has attained world renown. It is even listed as a Protected Urban Architectural Heritage Zone with the appropriate authorities. The flea market was born as a means of dodging a tax levied in the nineteenth century on merchandise entering Paris. At that time, ragpickers, vendors of scrap metal, and other street merchants stopped their pushcarts outside the city's fortifications, to avoid paying the tax. Gradually, they built somewhat more permanent stalls, similar to the flea market you see today. Currently, they are collected in some fifteen markets. Vernaison is the oldest (1885); Dauphine is the most recent. The antique dealers of the Marché Biron had formed their own company by 1925. Each of the markets operates differently and includes several dozen dealers. The flea market covers nearly twenty acres and some 2,000 dealers are registered there. In the aisles of the markets, some of which are covered, the stalls overflow with a variety of goodies: antique armchairs, wardrobes, statuettes, prints, clothing, costume jewelry, and notions, not to mention valuable museum pieces. There's something for every budget, which is, in fact, what makes the flea market so attractive. As you enter the market via the Porte de Saint-Ouen, make sure to visit the adorable little wisteria-covered houses on the Rue Paul-Bert. Each of them is full of surprises, and well worth exploring. Next, you'll come to the Marché Paul Bert, where all the hipster fashionistas and designers shop. You'll soon see why. Pierre Bazalgue has an enchanting collection of curiosities: glass bells, skeletons, and other treasures which could form the basis for an excellent Wunderkammer are available in

Les Puces de Saint-Ouen

231

abundance. You can also stroll over to the Marché Cambon and treat yourself to an old Vuitton trunk at Le Monde du Voyage, which sells vintage 1920s luggage. Then all you need is a transatlantic liner for your crossing. Shoppers seeking the mood which reigned before the flea market became respectable will adore the labyrinthine aisles of the Marché Vernaison, with its vendors of glassware and scientific equipment.

Les Puces de Saint-Ouen

233

Agapè
www.agapedeco.com
• 91, avenue Jean-Baptiste-Clément
92100 Boulogne-Billancourt
Tel. 01 47 12 04 88
Métro: Boulogne-Jean-Jaurès

À la Mine d'Argent
www.minedargent.com
• 108, rue du Bac, 7th
Tel. 01 45 48 70 68
Métro: Sèvres-Babylone

À l'Orientale
• Arcades du Palais-Royal
19-22, galerie de Chartres, 1st
Tel. 01 42 96 43 16
Métro: Palais-Royal-Musée-du-Louvre

Antiquités-Curiosités
• 62, boulevard de Ménilmontant, 20th
Tel. 06 83 12 70 75
Métro: Père-Lachaise

Antiquités Delacroix
• 67, place du Docteur-
Félix-Lobligeois, 17th
Tel. 01 42 29 31 36
Métro: Rome ou Brochant

As'Art
www.as-art.fr
• 3, passage du Grand-Cerf, 2th
Tel. 01 44 88 90 40
Métro: Étienne-Marcel
• 35, rue Saint-Paul, 4th
Tel. 01 48 04 58 41
Métro: Saint-Paul

Astier de Villatte
www.astierdevillatte.com
• 173, rue Saint-Honoré, 1st
Tel. 01 42 60 74 13
Métro: Tuileries or Palais-Royal-
Musée-du-Louvre
• 63, boulevard Masséna, 13th
Tel. 01 43 45 72 72
Métro: Porte-d'Ivry

Au Bon Usage
www.aubonusage.com
• 21, rue Saint-Paul, 4th
Tel. 01 42 78 80 14
Métro: Saint-Paul

Au Petit Bonheur
la Chance
• 13, rue Saint-Paul, 4th
Tel. 01 42 74 36 38
Métro: Saint-Paul

Au Présent du Passé
• 36, rue Davioud, 16th
Tel. 01 42 24 06 08
Métro: Ranelagh

Au Progrès

www.auprogres.net
• 11 bis, rue Faidherbe, 11th
Tel. 01 43 71 70 61
Métro: Faidherbe-Chaligny

Aux Salles de Bains rétro

www.sbrparis.com
• 27, rue Benjamin-Franklin, 16th
Tel. 01 47 27 14 50
Métro: Trocadéro
• 29-31, rue des Dames, 17th
Tel. 01 43 87 88 00
Métro: Place-de-Clichy

Aux Trois Singes

• 23, rue Saint-Paul, 4th
Tel. 01 42 72 73 69
Métro: Saint-Paul

Balouga

www.balouga.com
• 25, rue des Filles-du-Calvaire, 3th
Tel. 01 42 74 01 49
Métro: Filles-du-Calvaire

Belle Lurette

• 5, rue du Marché-Popincourt, 11th
Tel. 01 43 38 67 39
Métro: Parmentier

Brokatik

• 2, rue de l'Hôpital-Saint-Louis, 10th
Tel. 01 42 40 10 34
Métro: Gare-de-l'Est or
Colonel-Fabien

Caravane Chambre

www.caravane.fr
• 19, rue Saint-Nicolas, 12th
Tel. 01 53 02 96 96
Métro: Ledru-Rollin

Caravane Emporium

www.caravane.fr
• 22, rue Saint-Nicolas, 12th
Tel. 01 53 17 18 55
Métro: Ledru-Rollin

Carouche

www.carouche-typepad.com
• 18, rue Jean-Macé, 11th
Tel. 01 43 73 53 03
Métro: Charonne

Claude Nature

www.claudenature.com
• 32, boulevard Saint-Germain, 5th
Tel. 01 44 07 30 79
Métro: Maubert-Mutualité

Complément d'objet

www.complementdobjet.com
• 11, rue Jean-Pierre-Timbaud, 11th
Tel. 01 43 57 09 28
Métro: Oberkampf

Cuisinophilie

• 28, rue du Bourg-Tibourg, 4th
Tel. 01 40 29 07 32
Métro: Saint-Paul

Dans l'air du temps

• 12, rue Lacépède, 5th
Tel. 01 42 17 06 39
Métro: Place-Monge

De l'autre côté de la Butte

• 5, rue Muller, 18th
Tel. 01 42 62 26 06
Métro: Château-Rouge

Design & Things

www.alexislahellec.com
• 22, rue du Pont-Neuf, 1st
Tel. 01 42 33 41 25
Métro: Les Halles or Pont-Neuf

Deyrolle

www.deyrolle.fr
• 46, rue du Bac, 7th
Tel. 01 42 22 30 07
Métro: Rue-du-Bac

Et Puis c'est Tout

• 72, rue des Martyrs, 9th
Tel. 01 40 23 94 02
Métro: Pigalle

Fiesta

www.fiesta-galerie.fr
- 45, rue Vieille-du-Temple, 4th
Tel. 01 42 71 53 34
Métro: Saint-Paul

Fuchsia

- 2, rue de l'Ave-Maria, 4th
Tel. 01 48 04 75 61
Métro: Saint-Paul

Galerie Alexis Lahellec

www.alexislahellec.com
- 14-16, rue Jean-Jacques-
Rousseau, 1st
Tel. 01 42 33 36 95
Métro: Palais-Royal-Musée-du-Louvre
or Louvre-Rivoli

Galerie Dansk

www.galeriedansk.com
- 31, rue Charlot, 3rd
Tel. 01 42 71 45 95
Métro: Filles-du-Calvaire or Temple

Images et Portraits

- 35-37, rue Charlot, 3rd
(entry from 39, rue de Bretagne
as well)
Tel. 06 65 23 95 03
Métro: Filles-du-Calvaire or Temple

Jérôme Lepert

- 106, rue Vieille-du-Temple, 3rd
Tel. 06 10 18 18 88
Métro: Filles-du-Calvaire

Kin Liou

- 81, rue du Bac, 7th
Tel. 01 45 48 80 85
Métro: Rue-du-Bac
or Sèvres-Babylone

La Calinière

- 68, rue Vieille-du-Temple, 3rd
Tel. 01 42 77 40 46
Métro: Saint-Paul

La Maison

- 3, rue Neuve-Popincourt, 11th
Tel. 01 48 06 59 47
Métro: Parmentier

La Tortue Électrique

www.tortue-electrique.com
- 7, rue Frédéric-Sauton, 5th
Tel. 01 43 29 37 08
Métro: Maubert-Mutualité

Le Château de ma mère

- 108, avenue Ledru-Rollin, 11th
Tel. 01 43 14 26 03
Métro: Ledru-Rollin

Les Curieuses

www.lescurieuses.com
- 4, rue Oberkampf, 11th
Tel. 01 47 00 97 65
Métro: Filles-du-Calvaire

Les Frères Nordin

- 215, rue du Faubourg-
Saint-Antoine, 11th
Tel. 01 43 72 38 35
Métro: Faidherbe-Chaligny

Les Modernistes

www.lesmodernistes.com
- 2, rue Théophile-Roussel, 12th
Tel. 06 26 12 37 41
Métro: Ledru-Rollin

Les Portes du Monde

www.portesdumonde-paris.com
- 166, boulevard du
Montparnasse, 14th
Tel. 01 43 35 01 02
RER Port-Royal or Métro: Vavin

Les Puces de Saint-Ouen

www. parispuces.com
- Rues des Rosiers, Jules-Vallès,
Biron, Paul-Bert
93400 Saint-Ouen
Tel. 08 92 705 765
Métro: Porte-de-Saint-Ouen
or Porte-de-Clignancourt

Les Puces de Vanves
www.pucesdevanves.typepad.com
• Avenues Marc-Sangnier and Georges-Lafenestre, 14th
Métro: Porte-de-Vanves

Les Touristes
www.lestouristes.eu
• 17, rue des Blancs-Manteaux, 4th
Tel. 01 42 72 10 84
Métro: Hôtel-de-Ville

Le Temps Suspendu
• 103, rue du Théâtre, 15th
Tel. 01 45 75 80 67
Métro: La Motte-Picquet-Grenelle

L'Objet qui parle
• 86, rue des Martyrs, 18th
Tel. 06 09 67 05 30
Métro: Abbesses

L'Œil du Pélican
www.loeildupelican.fr
• 13, rue Jean-Jacques-Rousseau, 1st
Tel. 01 40 13 70 00
Métro: Palais-Royal-Musée-du-Louvre or Louvre-Rivoli

Loulou les Âmes Arts
• 104, quai de Jemmapes, 10th
Tel. 01 42 00 91 39
or 06 11 42 35 98
Métro: Jacques-Bonsergent

Masala
www.masala.fr
• 44, rue Monsieur-le-Prince, 6th
Tel. 01 56 24 11 47
RER Luxembourg or Métro: Odéon

Pages 50/70
www.pages50-70.com
• 15, rue Yvonne-Le-Tac, 18th
Tel. 01 42 52 48 59
Métro: Abbesses

Rarissime
• 18, rue Saint-Roch, 1st
Tel. 01 42 96 30 49
Métro: Pyramides or Tuileries

Rickshaw
www.rickshaw.fr
• 7, passage du Grand-Cerf, 2nd
Tel. 01 42 21 41 03
Métro: Étienne-Marcel

Rickshaw Textiles
www.rickshaw.fr
• 10, passage du Grand-Cerf, 2nd
Tel. 01 40 26 37 95
Métro: Étienne-Marcel

Tombées du camion
• 15-17, rue Joseph-de-Maistre, 18th
Tel. 06 62 07 20 87
Métro: Blanche

Trolls et Puces
• 1, rue du Marché-Popincourt, 11th
Tel. 01 43 14 60 00
Métro: Parmentier

Weber Métaux et Plastiques
www.weber-france.com
• 9, rue de Poitou, 3rd
Tel. 01 42 71 23 45
Métro: Filles-du-Calvaire
• 66, rue de Turenne, 3rd
Tel. 01 42 71 23 45
Métro: Filles-du-Calvaire
• 34, rue Maurice-Gunsbourg
94200 Ivry-sur-Seine
Tel. 01 46 72 34 00

XXO
www.xxo.com
• 78, rue de la Fraternité
93230 Romainville
Tel. 01 48 18 08 88

Zut
Frédéric Daniel Antiquités
www.antiquités-industrielles.com
• 7-9, rue Ravignan, 18th
Tel. 06 82 67 81 77
Métro: Abbesses

À la curiosité, moteur de toutes les passions, à celle
qui anime les gens que j'aime et à Tante Malène
qui sut éveiller la mienne quand j'étais enfant.
É. P.

Au brol de ma Youyou, qui m'a tant inspirée
À Philippe Peron, pour sa manière si bucolique de chiner
À ce plaisir toujours renouvelé de découvrir la beauté là
où on ne l'attend pas
À vous, objets délaissés, qui nous racontez
poétiquement des histoires.
S. A.

Call to mind the indescribable tingle of suspense aroused by the idea of that unexpected something that has been lying there, biding its time, waiting for you to find it. This list of 58 addresses will lead you to hidden discoveries, large and small, in the best vintage, antique, and collectibles shops all over the city of Paris. At the rear of a courtyard or sheltered by a 19th-century arcade, in a Gothic stone basement or in an ordinary looking shop, thousands of marvels await.

US $18.95 / £10.99 UK
ISBN 978-1-892145-73-4

THE LITTLE BOOKROOM
NEW YORK